A Boilermaker for the Lady

Also by Fred Yannantuono

Smack My Ass and Call Me Sally

A Boilermaker for the Lady

Fred Yannantuono

The New York Quarterly Foundation, Inc.
New York, New York

NYQ Books™ is an imprint of The New York Quarterly Foundation, Inc.

The New York Quarterly Foundation, Inc.
P. O. Box 2015
Old Chelsea Station
New York, NY 10113

www.nyqbooks.org

Copyright © 2009 by Fred Yannantuono

All rights reserved. No part of this book may be used or reproduced in any manner whatsoever without written permission of the author. This book is a work of fiction. Any references to historical events, real people or real locales are used fictitiously. Other names, characters, places, and incidents are products of the author's imagination, and any resemblance to actual events or locales or persons, living or dead, is entirely coincidental.

First Edition

Set in New Baskerville

Layout and Design by Raymond P. Hammond
Cover Photo by Fred Yannantuono

Library of Congress Control Number: 2009931574

ISBN: 978-1-935520-06-1

A Boilermaker for the Lady

Acknowledgments

Grateful acknowledgment is made to the editors of the following journals in which these poems, or previous versions, first appeared: "Big Joe & Sons," *Brooklyn Review*; "The Beautiful Error," *Cairn*; "I Hate to Second-Guess Myself, or Do I?" *Confrontation*; "A Boilermaker for the Lady," *CQ:California Quarterly*; "The Evil of Two Lessers," *Eclipse*; "Palindrome for an Average Player," *Eureka Literary Magazine*; "Grapefruit," "Lines Written While Adding Three Inches to My Penis," *Good Foot*; "Hands," *Green Hills Literary Lantern*; "Frog Pond," "One Less Thing to Think About," "There in the Citrus-Scented Air," "Three Clockmakers Fix My Clock," *Hampden-Sydney Poetry Review*; "De Troot," *The Hollins Critic*; "Smack My Ass and Call Me Sally," *Inkwell*; "Bean There, Done That," "Message in a Bottle Palindrome," "My Pastor Limerick," "Seaman Limerick," "Sonnet to Whatever It Is That Kills Porcupines," "The Thought of It," *Light Quarterly*; "The River of Forgetfulness," *Limestone*; "Death of an Olive," *Madison Review*; "Salt," *Massachusetts Review*; "Bath," *Meridian Anthology*; "Knife," "Piscataway," "She Wouldn't Say the Word Buffet," "This Is Phthisis," *The Mochila Review*; "Katabasis in Jag," *New Orleans Review*; "Canine Delusions of Grandeur Palindrome," "Cigars," "Gentlemen's Club Limerick," "Incest Palindrome," "Magritte's Palindrome," "On the Sixth Day Palindrome," "Sophisticated Courtship Palindrome," *New York Quarterly*; "I Miss the Time When There Was No Real World," *Old Red Kimono*; "And Our Brains Have Sailed Away," *Phoebe*; "It's Done, the Place Is Stripped," *Plainsongs*; "Boyshort $7.50 (from H & M)," "My Librarian Looks at Love," *Poem*; "White Christmas," *Quiddity*; "Grand Central," "Requiem for Two Cents," *Red Wheelbarrow*; "Biscuit Villanelle," *RiverSedge*; "Alcatraz," *Sulphur River*; "Interstices Limerick," *Westchester County Business Journal*; "83 Poems on Baking Bread," *West Wind Review*; "Amour Propre," *Willard & Maple*; "The Return of Madame La Hoya," *Willow Springs*.

This book is affectionately dedicated to everyone in the world except for my immediate family.

Contents

Cigars	13
I Miss the Time When There Was No Real World	14
My Librarian Looks at Love	15
Lines Written While Adding Three Inches to My Penis	17
Salt	18
Hands	19
Grand Central	20
Death of an Olive	22
Sonnet to Whatever It Is That Kills Porcupines	23
Katabasis in Jag	24
Grapefruit	25
Limericks	26
Message in a Bottle Palindrome	27
On the Sixth Day Palindrome	27
Palindrome for an Average Player	27
There in the Citrus-Scented Air	28
Amour Propre	29
Bean There, Done That	30
One Less Thing to Think About	31
The Evil of Two Lessers	32
83 Poems on Baking Bread	34
Piscataway	35
How Strange and Complete	36
The Thought of It	37
A Boilermaker for the Lady	38
Big Joe & Sons	39
More Limericks	42
Incest Palindrome	43
Canine Delusions of Grandeur Palindrome	43
Ugandan Palindrome	43
Riggins	44
Refresh My Mammary, Ohne Büstenhalter	45
This Is Phthisis	46
I Hate to Second-Guess Myself, or Do I?	47

River Lure	48
She Wouldn't Say the Word Buffet	49
Requiem for Two Cents	50
Knife	51
Pebbles	52
Frog Pond	53
The River of Forgetfulness	54
Prayer to the Moon	56
Biscuit Villanelle	57
Smack My Ass and Call Me Sally	58
Boyshort $7.50 (from H&M)	59
Three Clockmakers Fix My Clock	60
Scouring	62
Resurrection	63
Alcatraz	64
Frozen Pose	65
White Christmas	66
And Our Brains Have Sailed Away	67
Even More Limericks	68
Magritte's Palindrome	69
Sophisticated Courtship Palindrome	69
Philanderer's Palindrome	69
De Troot	70
It's Done, the Place Is Stripped	71
Bargeman	72
Too Few	73
The Beautiful Error	74
Bath	75
Until You Seduce a Lesbian, You'll Never Be Updike	76
The Return of Madame La Hoya	77

A Boilermaker for the Lady

CIGARS

> *Remember the moon and the stars, and all those nights we smoked cigars.*
> —Jackie Gleason

At twelve o'clock we broke out the cigars,
Poured ourselves a shot to loose the tongue,
And lay beneath a flowerbed of stars.

We'd barhopped in your classic teenage car,
Conjured girls we'd known when we were young,
Then closed things down and broke out the cigars.

Sure, we'd bobbled things—the seminars
Of failure—youth! Miscues unsung stung
Us there beneath the flowerbed of stars.

Yet nothing nightly lately nearly mars
The fluid Cuban storytelling wrung
Perfecto when you break out the cigars.

Life, death—midnight's isobars
In undulating smoke rings, floating, hung
Coronal on the flowerbed of stars.

Awash in Time's bright distant avatars,
To smoke and probe the stuff we're made among—
At twelve o'clock we broke out the cigars
And lay beneath a flowerbed of stars.

I MISS THE TIME WHEN THERE WAS NO REAL WORLD

I miss the time when there was no real world,
Just the three of us in our small boat,
Running with the tide as words unfurled.

When I told you stories, your toes curled
Beneath you, drawbridges from moats.
I miss the time when there was no real world.

We were troubadours. Words swirled
Onstage in plays which we cowrote.
Running with the tide, the words unfurled.

Your smiled defiances theatrically hurled—
Even those we took as a grace note.
Amiss the time misspent in the real world.

Lying on our bellies, inklings twirled,
Wreathing round the future's asymptote,
Running on the tide as words unfurled.

You, my beauties, souls impearled
In wording, take this as a quote:
I miss the time when there was no real world,
Running with the tide as words unfurled.

MY LIBRARIAN LOOKS AT LOVE

Love, turtledove's,
In the looks,
In the steams
Of your dreams,
In the smells
Of the swells,
Not the books.
Things that matter—
How to flatter,
Countercoups,
Billets-doux.
Arms enwreathing,
Limbs unsheathing,
Legs entwining,
Light declining.
You alone,
Sweet molasses?
Gotta moan,
Shuck the glasses.

In the stacks
Romance lacks.
Feelings taper
While on paper.
Heavy breathing?
Lovelorn seething?
Who can name it?
They all claim it.

First there's Suckling.
Mere unbuckling.

Shakespeare's carriage
Ends in marriage.
Stop that frowning,
E.B. Browning.
Can one learnest
Aught from Ernest?
Henry Miller?
There's a killer.

Nothing warrants
D.H. Lawrence:
Kisses tender?
Yes, but gender!
All those theses,
Exegeses.
Stick to sex—
Less complex.

In the stacks
Romance lacks.
In the light
Blood takes flight.
Down below
Tales of woe.
Up above
Ha ha, love!

LINES WRITTEN WHILE ADDING
THREE INCHES TO MY PENIS

Every time I go online I'm told to do this. But I have questions.
If they add three to me, will that subtract three from somebody else?
Will it be in a straight line and, if so, which end do they plan to add
the inches to? They often say *women agree, size does count.*
Does this include the ones that I meet in church? Why do women
get these messages too? Will I always have three more inches
or will it depend on the time of day? With three more inches,
will the extra blood that rushes to them cause me to pass out
at inconvenient times? Will the three inches be made up by
compensation in breadth, like a rubber band being stretched out?
How do they know I don't want to shorten it? The women I've met
all say the shorter the better, yet none of them has ever been interviewed.
How did they settle on three? Why is that better than adding
two inches to your penis or, say, one-and-a-half?
If three is good, what about four? Why is nature providing
so many of us with minus three inches? Why haven't we evolved
the other three, or have women only started demanding them lately?
Are the people sending me these messages the same ones telling me
I ought to get breast implants? If they know that my penis is
three inches short, why don't they know that my breasts are
exactly the right size or maybe a bit too big, thank you very much?
If men who have already added three inches to their penises
are sending these messages and they believe women prefer this,
isn't this dumb of them? If women are sending these messages,
why don't they call me direct? I'm hoping hermaphrodites
aren't sending these messages, but so far I can't rule it out.

SALT

When you speak I salt your words,
patting them down and wrapping them
carefully in the black skins of yams,
laying them crosshatch for transport
in the mind's hold, so fresh, so
perishable I have no choice
but to cure them like herring or cod.

In your mouth—in my mouth—they are
too fresh and perishable. There is so much
taste that the mind becomes peppered,
encouraged to roam between meanings.
Laid down, salted, and cured, I can have them
when I'm hungry; there is less meaning then
and it's fixed, but what little there is is
digestible, satisfying enough, and will keep.

HANDS

At what age would I want you back?
At forty, when your rough hand
Cupped mine like a husk on a
Nut, I tugging at your ear, laughing,
As you pretended to lunch on my belly
Like a lion on his kill?
At sixty, when your rueful eyes
Accepted without question
The spear of separation
With a handshake and a smile?
At seventy, when you quietly asked if I were sure,
And hearing linnets, accepted unconditionally
The screech of starlings?
At eighty-nine, when you startled me by
Rising from your sleep
To tell me she'd be back?

Peter came to visit and we held your hands.
Your grip was like a blacksmith's.
You were, I realize, many men,
All forged in tenderness and strength.
Three years now, at ninety-two,
You're gone.

I'd like you back at all times.
I want the basement door to slam,
To hear the light switch on,
To hear your step on the basement stairs,
To see your hand emerge along the banister.

GRAND CENTRAL

The Harlem Line leads straight from here to Bronxville.
While I wait, I buy a can of beer.
That's what I drink while I'm waiting here
When I'm tired of wandering through the city,
Killing time while waiting in the station,
Browsing in the bookstore through the literary world.

I don't know the literary world.
I'm no longer sure I know my Bronxville.
I don't know if knowing is my station—
Students growing up and drinking beer.
No one knows enough about the city,
Just the here and now, the mostly here.

All my life, I've railed it home from here.
O to such a pleasant little world!
Lapidary green, unlike the city.
Nothing means so much to me as Bronxville,
Especially when I've drunk a little beer,
Which I drink while waiting in the station.

Now I see the train is in the station,
Track change signals, track 12 boarding here.
I think that I could use another beer.
Get me to that pleasant little world
Where I've lived so long, my little Bronxville.
Filling up with upstarts from the city.

Always when I'm visiting the city
I accept the presence of the station,
How it waits to take me back to Bronxville,
How I end up gravitating here.
New York is a slightly bigger world,
Bitterer than Bronxville or the beer.

Yes, I'll buy another can of beer.
I can't wait to get out of the city.
Take me to my lapidary world.
Start me chuffing northward through the station.
Get me whistling through the Bronx from here.
Get me headed straight back home to Bronxville.

Bless the beer in Grand Central station!
Bless the city, though it's bitter here!
Bless the little world I have in Bronxville!

DEATH OF AN OLIVE

O vile
O evil
olive!
Slain oval,
you matte-drab
deserved
it. De-vined,
minced-mottled
for tapénade—
or pitted,
pimentoed,
brine-bottled,
you're *not alive*!
Evil? A ton.
O voile pearl
in gin oyster,
O livid,
sipped or
nibbled
memento
redolent
of vine,
of veiled and
short-lived
love.
Ave atque vale,
O vile
O evil
olive!

SONNET TO WHATEVER IT IS THAT KILLS PORCUPINES

A porcupine's an iffy thing to kill.
It's not an easy concept to intuit.
Be honest. How would you attempt to do it?
The iron macaroni of the quill.

I've read about a mammal that can do it.
It's quite a feat that's given it its fame.
The trouble is, I can't recall its name
Or how it gets the upper hand. O screw it—

It's stealthy, little, lithe, astute, and game.
Its work involves deception, unawares,
As Porky pines Petunia often swears
A nose by any otter smells the same.

Nor badger, weasel, skunk, nor wolverine—
Along those lines but somewhere in between.

KATABASIS IN JAG

What you gain is a quick piece of fish
Poorly prepared, let's say inedible,
But you're hungry.
You're poor too, down to
Two point three if you cash in now,
Which could be tricky.
You gain Euro tunes, a prick of a
Mixmaster dispensing found brands of
Retro-effrontery, anonymity, a loyal
Horse-faced boob pledged to a nasty abuser,
Two beauties spending way too much time
Sifting through tunes on a halter-top high jukebox,
The brunette of which you'd give your
Titanium eye-teeth implants for if the
Prick poured you one more ounce of Chivas
Without having to be asked.
And a host of Eucharistic possibilities.

Ah, but what you lose! Biblical sole from
Acid Al, Andy's majestic Scotch sours,
The courtship of an artichoke
As George cajoles the duck—
Duck, you're going to die—
Blueberries with Eddie whose static lips hail
Hail-fellow Jim whose hernia burst,
Teddy's booming punch lines
When—*annus mirabilis!*—the bolthole gapes
And Mulligan the Juggernaut,
Straight from the Two Man March,
Blasts in to cleanse the world
Of falsity and cant.
Brunetteless, you gasp, and fall face first
Into the suck and comfort of
A double decaf Jamaica Jamoc.
How can one replicate that?

Behind you the past slips away.
Before you the fog bank approaches.

GRAPEFRUIT

Your lips educe
The sections of
Grapefruit I bit into
At noon, after laboriously
Thumbing off rind and
Peel and touching them
Idly. They parted and
Slaked a thirst
I've had for a long, long time.

I was like you once,
Lying to everyone, wanting,
Wanting what I wanted,
What everyone wants
Who's felt a thirst in
This warm orchard:
To lie to you and
Attain your hair and
Part your lips, which are
The sections of grapefruit
I bit into at noon.

LIMERICKS

Pedicures! God, they're effete!
Fiddling around with your feet.
If you can't procure
A good manicure,
This is the way to defeat.

I hope I'm not out of the loop
In worshipping Bacciagalupe.
And I'm in the habit
Of worshipping Abbott—
Hillary, Sidney, the group.

A seaman who ate his clams raw
Was tempted to try something more.
Though not touchy-feely,
He fondled scungilli,
Unheard of in maritime law.

I used to think it was a crock
This blaming things on writer's block
Till, nothing igniting,
I'm forcing the writing
And everything comes out as schlock.

MESSAGE IN A BOTTLE PALINDROME

Tortuga's murder. Heave ho! Tosspots parted it. Pirates! Yo! Ha! Avast! It's Ava! Ahoy! Set a rip tide trap. Stops sot. Oh *Eva*, eh? Red rum's a gut-rot.

ON THE SIXTH DAY PALINDROME

God tackles ibis, elk, cat, dog.

PALINDROME FOR AN AVERAGE PLAYER

Tennis. A lob? A rap? O, no. Parabolas in net.

THERE IN THE CITRUS-SCENTED AIR

Every time I pass there by the stair
I'm whisked to the fan chair on the Isle of Bones—
We're there, in the citrus-scented air.

Mickey's cherry shorts, his cheery air,
His three thumbs waving like a metronome
Every time I pass there by the stair.

The salvage of the *Swallow, Wrecked*, beware!
That tree house was our home away from home—
There in the citrus-scented air.

Your beach chair draped in towels in the glare,
Papa's catwalk, mangos, palindromes,
Every time I pass there by the stair.

His worried eyes, your highlit, salt-laced hair,
Your wet suit's blackness, reef fish, ocher tones—
There, in the citrus-scented air.

Now the distant sloop will bear us there,
Will navigate the waters of a poem.
Every time I pass there by the stair—
We're there, in the citrus-scented air.

AMOUR PROPRE

The dumbest guy in thirty years and we're
alone in the warehouse and I guess he's got
a chain-gang background cause he's barking
out *Yes, Boss! Yes, Boss!* every time I tell him
what to do, and it starts to get on my nerves so
I tell him *Do me a favor, Robert, don't call me
boss. Call me numbnuts, cause that's what I've got
to be to be working in a place like this.*

It's more than a joke. He could be the dumbest guy
in *sixty* years, and he's still got to back off
with something like *Boss, I can't do that.*

Instead, he comes alive, and with great gusto
starts shouting out *Yes, numbnuts!* every time
I tell him what to do. It's got a certain sting to it—
I start to think of telling him to shove it.
Then I lighten up—it frees me being told by
the dumbest guy in thirty years that I'm
a numbnuts every time I tell him what to do.
He and I get used to the routine.

Next day, everybody's there and I'm barking
out orders and he's shouting out *Yes, numbnuts!*
every time I tell him what to do.
A pall spreads over the workforce.

BEAN THERE, DONE THAT

When it comes to making chili
I do something some think silly.
Briefly, I don't know the meaning
Of toning down the beaning.

Garbanzo, pinto, Orson, soy
Throw 'em in there. Boy O boy!
Navy, fava, black, frijol—
Any fruit raised on a pole.

Jumping, kidney, lima, green,
Beans are holy in between
Tomatoes peppered in the pot—
Jalapeños? Hot's what you got.

When it's done, congratulations!
Onward toward the flatulations!

ONE LESS THING TO THINK ABOUT

There's the glass of cabernet,
the cheapo, black-band Timex,
a, thank God, expanse of chest
in a horripilating lime-green Polo,
forearms like Popeye's, and the pad,
the pen, the cherry wood.

But no head. The writer, decapitate,
wonders what to use for cogitation—
the heart, plump pump, whose thrum
he must have listened to before?
The lungs, kiting words into the air?
The kidneys, clarifying, clarifying?
His trouble-making, problematic parts?
What about his bile, his gall—
a writer's knives? What are they
compared to the gaffes, the slips,
the fuzzy imprecisions of the head?

The writer decides it is better
not to have a head for all the good
it does. The pen descends and
blue ink disembogues, flushing
everything, lime rinds in an ashtray,
the raw bar's vellum-bound
Kiplings, the zinc catch basin,
this year's flowerless gowns,
into one upholstered river.

THE EVIL OF TWO LESSERS
The people have spoken. The bastards.
—Mark Twain

1992
I couldn't bring myself to vote for Bill.
Hub of Hill.
Nor for Bush.
Brain of mush.
Instead I drank a bottle of merlot
And voted for Perot.

1996
Again I couldn't pull the chain for Bill.
Blither still.
Nor for Dole.
Vacuole.
I drank another bottle of merlot
And voted for Perot.

2000
I couldn't bring myself to vote for Gore.
Temple whore.
Nor for Bush.
Brain of mush.
Laughs galore, Bush and Gore—
I sought the truth
And weighed her.
I polished off a magnum of merlot
And reached the Nader.

2004
Then I had the chance to vote for Kerry.
Warrior cherry.

Or for Bush.
Brain of mush.
When all is said and done one must be fair.
What's the truth and
Who mislaid her?
I drank another magnum of merlot.
Again for Nader.

2008
Now I've had the chance to vote Obama:
Dalai Lama.
John McCain:
Royal pain.
That Palin gal,
Who *made* her?
I conjure up a jeroboam of merlot.
Once more for Nader.

The End
I'd have gladly
Gone for Bradley.
Or for Kemp.
(Even Shemp).
Or for Udall
By them wooed all.
Grit detected.
None selected.
Hearty parties
Party farty.
I sometimes wonder how it sank so low.
Time for one last bottle of merlot.

83 POEMS ON BAKING BREAD
In all honesty, it pays to have a theme.
—Poetry contest prize judge

Or monastic living, say,
Where every day's a challenge.
The problem of food—
Take bread, for instance.
Say you're hungry, there's no variety.
Same old single grain
Beaten, kneaded with a wooden spoon
    Who cares if God loves me?
He or She, particularly She, must
Find her fey and portentous, cranking out
    83 pages of what she fervidly believes will rise as verse
On bread
Which you can't get the smell of into words,
And you've got to slather something on to bring out the flavor of.
But in her eight-by-ten-foot cell with the four-inch stone
Pillow
The best condiments are her dreams
    Which aid the mastication of the breadstuff
Spoon-fed to the limpid, gaga judge
Metronomically *famished* in Connecticut,
In hock to poetical powers,
Overworked and overweight and comfy with a theme—
Just bad enough to have been considered good for the job,
Pencilled in as yeast
In a rising tract
On bread.

PISCATAWAY

> *Gober crafts his objects by hand to serve as*
> *metaphors for human existence.*
>   —SFMOMA on Gober's "Two Urinals"

I too would craft urinals by hand,
lovingly sculpting spacious basins
en passant, neither of which would
be superfluous. And not out of specious
plastic either—out of marble, obsidian,
lapis lazuli, something sapid and eternal,
perhaps with a delicate piscine motif
boldly plastered on American Standard.

Being an artist can be so supposititious.
To trod the path of a day's inspiration
and not have recourse to a spiffy pissoir
hand-turned by a wiz with éclat and
pizzazz who's plumbed man's mind
in all of its liquid epistemology—
how piss-poor is that?

Creating can be suspiciously insipid.
My pieces are passing fancies, his as
appeasing as episiotomies, but with
the pomp and passion, the pith and
paste, of a Dear John letter from Paris,
or even Piscataway.

HOW STRANGE AND COMPLETE

How strange and complete it was to hear
That he'd been fired, then that he had died.
When were we notified—was it a month, a year?
Youth—yes, youth tripped him up, youth uneyed.

Just an old man struggling to make ends meet.
We'd hopped the fence and slid under the sailfishes,
Heard the watchman scrape of his booted feet,
Blind and hawk-eyed youth sating its wishes.

What were the odds the old man had to beat
To thwart the cylinders of the swift and rich?
Just an old man struggling to make ends meet,
Not mouthing off to fate, the bitch,

Who, squaring things, will do the same for me
When I'm old and stiff, struggling to make ends meet,
Out and about, pushing eighty-three,
As capable as he, as obsolete.

THE THOUGHT OF IT

There's one thing, darling dearest, which I will never do.
I'll never wear a certain kind of shoe.
I gave the things a trial run thirty years ago.
I can't recall what prompted me—was going with the flow.
I put them on. I took a step. I took them off real quick.
A most disgusting bellyache—it nearly made me sick.
If forced to dance a conga line through hellfire's hottest throes
I wouldn't put on sandals with straps between the toes.

It's not that I'm so ticklish. It wasn't that it hurt.
But something in it made my mind shift into high alert.
The thought of it. The thought of it. Enough to make one sick.
I can't describe my reasoning. I took them off real quick.
I can't describe the reasoning that went into the hate.
The ickiness. The ickiness. On this there's no debate.

I know that millions wear them, but if you took a poll
You'd find one man against them from the bottom of his soul.
You'd find a man against them who, if given half the chance,
Would celebrate toes' separateness, like legs upon a pants.
For feet were not designed for things like mittens or a glove.
The space between the toes was chiseled out by God above.
I'm sorry, darling dearest. It's Birkenstocks, or hose—
I love you, but it grieves me when you wear a pair of those.

A BOILERMAKER FOR THE LADY

In an affair of the heart
it doesn't do to ask too many questions.
You saw for yourself what she looks like,
a black rose clipped from an iron hedge.
If I told you I'd been in her room
what would you say?
True. That too. A coup.
How strange to be able to say
I could be in Las Hermanas by dawn.

So who is svelte Elena stewing in the drive?
How does the poster of Carter
jibe with the philoprogenitive itch?
How philadelphic can I be
without planting a kiss on you?
A smile bestowed on everyone
releases all from debt.
Hear the whir of Valkyries.
Bethink yourself of Rosalind or Kate.
You don't know the half of this.
Neither do I.

BIG JOE & SONS

O wielder of the needle and flame,
You, Joe, pointillist, scorer,
Scarificator of epiderma,
Cataractal etcher of acrid,
Blackened, red and blue demons
For hard-drinking, skin-scotched,
Harley-driving hellions
Named Flash, Nightstick,
And the hellcat Lady.
God dare not condemn you.

Jason died of diabetes
In a car in a 7-Eleven.
They thought him drunk
So left him.
Junior, twelve,
Has a face like a block of gneiss,
Can drive that bike in an
Ever-narrowing spiral
Like light spilling down
An imploding star,
Kicking up dirt like a
Maniacal, chiseled
Midget.

You, though, worry about
The neighborhood,
The pink pills at the phone booth,
The fuzzy hometown deals,
So you fling down Flash
Like Thor from Valhalla
To visit them with brimstone and

Pound a little sense into the boys.
Your walls are scarred with grotesques.
Your cabinets lined with the skulls
Of wolverines and bobcats.
An iguana, trancelike, inhabits the cage
In the foyer to the ladies' room,
Whose toilet rains down sludge
On Albie's workroom table
With clock-like regularity.
What primal nightmare leached its poison
To the river of crap you swim in day and night?

If *I* were a Jew and I had you
For a son,
I would be constantly laughing,
My thoughts so combustible
That Hegel or Kant
Would quail before me.
I would know that God
Is tattooed
And utterly helpless
In quarters.
I would look at your mother
With the look that
Joseph leveled at the
Parthenogenic Mary.

When you told me I must wait
Because the safe had been
Turned to the wall for
Fear of entry,
I was too amused to speak.

I can't speak now
Since I stood and took it then.
I applaud your
Words and your
Use of them.
For I feel your intentions are good.
I believe everything you say.

You are a big
Man who has eaten rat
And endured
Several courses of
Penicillin.

If what you say is true,
If life is as you prick it,
How can you be sure
That Jason won't return,
That Adam won't replace him,
That you yourself won't die,
That Gina won't suffer a relapse,
That the Cuban cigars won't actually
Come from Connecticut,
That the cod on the outer banks
Won't continue to show in your freezer,
That life itself won't vomit you up
Onto some sulfurous shore
Littered with needles and trusting, shaven youth,
Where your flowing hair
And necessitous eyes,
Your hulking, convivial form
Would be evermore sanctified
By ink and possession?

MORE LIMERICKS

When I get a note from a creditor
I'm not even sure if I've read it or
Imagined the bill—
Its tone is so shrill.
I'm forced to substantially edit her.

Once in an apotheosis
The Lord entered me by osmosis.
He made me so good
I'm now misunderstood:
Corporeal misdiagnosis.

My doctorate drained me. No fooling.
The constant redacted retooling.
Defending your diss
You fixate on this:
A fish can get tired of schooling.

Poetry's part of the nexus
Of that which unites us with Texas
Remember the Alamo
Is no shabby *mal à môt*.
But Travis and Crockett's cathexis.

INCEST PALINDROME

Dad's eye, Mom's eye, sis's eye eyes sis, eyes Mom, eyes Dad.

CANINE DELUSIONS OF GRANDEUR PALINDROME

Dog? I? Me? *Demigod!*

UGANDAN PALINDROME

To Idi Amin I'm a idiot.

RIGGINS

> *Riggins's nightlife drew as much attention as his on-field exploits. In 1985, at a Washington Press Club dinner, an intoxicated Riggins infamously told Supreme Court Justice Sandra Day O'Connor: "Come on, Sandy Baby, loosen up. You're too tight," then passed out on the floor.*
> —Wikipedia

Not quite. He winked, rose from
his seat, strode into the aisle, sat,
then lay full-length, immaculate in his
tuxedo, his face glazed, his arms
crossed on his chest,
nodding off serenely.
It was the act of a demigod,
of one in complete control.
Babe Ruth could have done it.
Gandhi, Caligula.
They laughed when they saw him,
all those tuxedos swaying in place
like so many penguins,
everyone but he, the horse led into
the Senate by his own hand, he his own
favorite horse. What did he dream of?
Beer? The slant left? Shakespeare? Pasadena?
He started to snore. Even the speaker
thought it rich. Riggins. Who else?
Over the top, flat on his back at the Press Club.

REFRESH MY MAMMARY, OHNE BÜSTENHALTER

She's got a balcony you could do Shakespeare from.
—Firesign Theater

Unburdened from some nameless bra
A whit of tit is it pour moi.
Let them resemble petits pois.
That's the max que je veux voir.

THIS IS PHTHISIS
Latin from Greek from phthinein *to waste away*

This phthisis—
Is it
Thigh, sis,
Tie, sis,
Or is this
This is?
Fthisis.
Phthisis?
What this is
Amiss is.

I HATE TO SECOND-GUESS MYSELF, OR DO I?

Then all at once I notice how your eyes,
Inclined in wine to blur the telltale flutter,
Insinuate in your old childhood stutter—
I hate to second-guess myself, or do I?

The kill of memory, trickling as it sings,
Broadens nightly to a roaring stream down
Which you lightly pole the muffled scream
Mothered in the fluttering of wings.

I hate to second-guess myself, or do I?
But where's the hand placed gently on the shoulder?
Where's the word to comfort growing older?
Where's the heart? Who hardened it? And why?

Here's to life up north among the lichen,
Always perfect form, without a twinge—
Perfect. Not the slightest flinch to hinge
On what you cooked up in your frigid kitchen.

Watching you, I have to wonder why
You think you have it corked up in a bottle,
Your ghost ship's grim, swift, supposititious model.
You clearly second-guess yourself. So should I?

Sitting there among your clutch of cats
In static silent splendor in the sprawling
Horsey fencey country, something's calling,
Never knowing right from wrong, and that

I like to think will, when your night is nigh
And, short of breath, but loath to leave behind
What breath you have, haunt you, panicked,
Looking up to find—
I hate to second-guess myself, or do I?

RIVER LURE

Teased hair piled high
(Up to a mile!)
A tap on the shirtsleeve,
A low tidal smile.
I feel the tug of a river lure's guile.

Colloguing on cranial portion
And shape,
Revealing a picturesque shot of the nape.
Yes, dissing the boyfriend
(That big hairy ape!)
I feel the tug of a river man's jape.

Eventually bearing the navy bean soup
While yakking my ear off
(I'm forced to regroup).
The hair spray, the nail job,
The laundry bin scoop.
I feel the tug of a riverboat sloop.

I cough up the greenbacks I got from the bank
And raise up my hand to propel her a thank.
She's got shapely withers
(You'd sure love to spank!)
I feel the tug of a riverboat prank.

SHE WOULDN'T SAY THE WORD BUFFET

She wouldn't say the word buffet.
She said she wanted proof
That if she did she wouldn't say
Such things as opera bouffe.

Her mother laughed to think of how
She wouldn't say the word buffet.
Her father wouldn't disavow
That if she did she wouldn't say

Bouffant. In weighing why and when
Her mother laughed to think of how
The word buffet could add an "n"
Her father wouldn't disavow.

Others chimed in, thought it strange—
Bouffant—in weighing why and when
When all you do is rearrange
The word buffet and add an "n."

She thought it a polite rebuff.
Others chimed in, thought it strange
To think buffet was quite enough
When all you do is rearrange

The notion of what you can say.
She thought it a polite rebuff.
She wouldn't say the word buffet.
To think buffet was quite enough.

REQUIEM FOR TWO CENTS

Someone said they used to call you Two Cents.
A paper cost that much back then. You'd wait till
someone else had coughed it up, scanned news,
checked sports, chucked it on the counter of the
seedy deco diner you cadged coffee in before
pretending to go out and look for work. Life was
sweet—you'd saved yourself two cents.

Your brother slipped you fiver after fiver,
most of them diverted from my pocket. In theory
you were kin—the set of the mouth, the cleft
of the chin. Not the eyes, though. Yours were slits.

The time we needed backup, he wouldn't make the call.
So I did, being wet behind the ears. The testy little no—
you'd made the touch. Handout after handout
down through the years meant nothing to a man
so rich in shtick.

In some thematic twining, you die the night I
first feel deathly ill. Stretched a hundred years,
a strand will snap.

I edge up to the coffin, pretending to pray, and,
when no one's looking, slip in the coins. This
feels better than expected. This makes me feel like
a million bucks. Buy yourself the rag down there,
you cheap son of a bitch who lived to be a hundred.
Requiescat in pennies.

KNIFE

Knife, thrown end over
   end, slows as if headed
      into wind, stops midair.

Why is it there? Is this
   what it seems? It could
      be a dream.

It should be a dream—
   frozen in light, knife
      reassessing flight.

PEBBLES

> *Demosthenes often recited poems while running up and down the sand dunes.*
> — Jan Strydom

I tried it once to see how it felt.
It was more or less like a heart attack.
Then I thought maybe *Howl* was the wrong approach
So I switched to *Sonnets from the Portuguese*.
No good—I noticed my hands were getting splotchy.
Slumping down, I jumped back up and did *September 1, 1939* at full tilt
Till I tripped on some sea grape and banged my knee
And said *d...d...d...d...damn!*

FROG POND

You see, to have frogs you've got to provide them
with water, which means pipes, which can run into
sprinklers. It helps, then, to have a gardener whose
gnarled, irrigational hands will make the place
hospitable to succulent slugs and crickets.

And rankness, murk—enclosed, putrescent. The smells
the oils of landscape, struggle, iodine. The sounds
atonally bubbling up out of the pipes, well or ill-laid
depending upon the skill of the gardener.

The line of the plants must be clean—spatterdock,
lotus, lily—or the lime-green scum on the rocks that
form the bank, the blue-green berries of the chinquapin,
caltrop, ornamental edging, the lacquered blur of fish
wheeling about like comets untethered in a small and
uncontrollable virulent universe.

It helps, too, to stock it with newts, or efts, to do
the reading required to stock the proper proportion
of goldfish, newts, and efts.

Most ominously, you've got to possess the time,
time in hand at the shank of the day to exit from the
portal of your two point eight six Tudor, break away
from the bits and PCs of your exophthalmic life
and traipse sweatily downhill to the pond.

Already you're uncomfortable thinking about it,
about the money, the gardener, the rankness, the murk,
the lack of a guarantee that there's anything valuable
about frog ponds in the first place, the thought that
while you're traipsing downhill with your heirs
and consigns in their little pink jumpers and OshKosh
B'Gosh, a deal may be tanking in Cleveland that
requires your hot-wired presence—which is why you
pay a mason to cart in half a ton of gravel and dump
it down and fill it in and solve the problem forever.

THE RIVER OF FORGETFULNESS

Praying over Rocco, laid notably out before me in his best
rococo finery, the brushed wool suit with stickpinned tie,
a soccer ball by his side, the sad cops and wired firemen
filing past him toward his spacey, corpulent sons and his
lynx-eyed, accountable womenfolk, I recall how, glimpsing
me past the hood of the hissing dishwasher, he bloomed like all
the rest of the shrinking violets, time out of mind, who've ever
levitated at a boss's reappearance. This time he is inert.

And then Marie, whose children had her cremated. In place of
the great rouged proof of transubstantiation, a mauve thing
the size of a toaster holds what's been rendered unto God.
I flinch to think of flesh in marble thuribles, and powdered
bones run against my grain. I see mine laid out in turf in some
fine field, or barring that, adjacent to the curb where I touch down.

I pull into The Swan to have a drink. You need a drink on a two-
wake night. And up and down the bar I have my thoughts. Crows.
Yeats. The Irish girls in March. Steve who does the cooking's
not around. I ask for him—I like his surly glare. Borrowing
a pen, I scribble thoughts on Rocco and Marie. The maitre d'
appears and says Steve's dead.

It's not that *I'd* deserve a long cortège. I've slain, once, mindlessly;
lied some, sometimes grievously; been grossly insensitive to
minimalists and all manner of Nazi. On the clearest day I could
never tell a donkey from an elephant.

They're all dead who would have mourned me best: Dachy,
who lived to countermand me; Jessie, whose blaze blurred like
a run-on crucifix; Pluto, who taught me how to read the Sunday
funnies under inlaid walnut end tables—all gone before me
to their preordained and retromingent permutations.

When I die they're going to fling up the sash and throw
my fucking body in the street. No harps, no hymns,
no psalms, nobody quoting Luke or spitting out encomiums
past clenched teeth. No bougainvillaea. A lonely course
commands a bitter cup: fleabane, lethe, an end to it.

PRAYER TO THE MOON

O moon, O mother moon,
Sailing through the slipstream of the stars,
Spin me on your orrery and rings
In your pale protectorate of bars.

O moon, O mother moon,
Imbue me with your elemental light,
Barge me on the flood tide you propel
Westward on your scepter of the night.

O moon, O mother moon,
Tapestries of cloud obscure your brow.
Riddle them with moonbeams, trim the jib,
Dim the constellations o'er your prow.

BISCUIT VILLANELLE

O how I hate her howling in the dark!
A man can only stand so much chanteuse.
I wish I had a dog that wouldn't bark.

I hate it when she piddles in the park,
Or makes me use the scooper—that's abuse.
Sheer hell to hear that howling in the dark!

Without a hound my life would be a lark.
She ate *Art Digest* right up to Toulouse-.
I'd grovel for a dog that wouldn't bark.

Politically her sympathy's with Marx,
Karl, or is that Groucho? She's abstruse.
Incessantly the howling in the dark!

It's gotten so she drinks my Cutty Sark.
I'd like to smack her right on the caboose.
I'd kill to have a dog that wouldn't bark.

Hounds exist to make you toe the mark.
I'd swap her for a wombat or a moose.
She'll kill me with that howling in the dark.
I wish I had a dog that wouldn't bark.

SMACK MY ASS AND CALL ME SALLY

Two demented Cajuns, me, an island girl who can't count up to three.

—Roger French

Quite the evening here at Hey José's and
here's a cheery thought. I can't recall
the last time I had sex. Not the month.
Not the year. Are you ready for this?
Not the decade. The purple lava lamp
shaped like a rocket isn't helping. Nor
the margarita. Before me mental nourishment:
a panoply of chili pepper bottles, some of which
they've used in the burritos: *Big Blaaster,
Hot Bitch at the Beach, Kiss Your Ass Goodbye,
Red Rectum, Screaming Sphincter, Anal
Armageddon, Lawyer's Breath,* and my personal
favorite, *Smack My Ass and Call Me Sally.*
It's all downhill from here to the ultimate
shooter, so I order a third burrito and
purchase one *Smack My Ass* (sale price $7.95)
for a gourmand friend who's headed to gourmet.
A tiny sober voice suggests it's time to switch
to ice cream. Quite the evening here at Hey José's.
Solo, sexless, piquant—with a crackling dawn
assured.

BOYSHORT $7.50 (FROM H & M)

Nor boy nor short, this shocking babe
in breezy bra and rocket briefs, teeth
lined up like twelve white guns, braided
hair splayed out like auburn snakes, with a
perfect little mole on a perfect little cheek.
I wonder what she'd think if she were here,
sitting in her cable stitch, swaddled in an
anorak, drinking herself in.

Do models think? I'm sure that on some level,
perhaps profoundly, they process many types of
complicated thought—hot and cold, yes and no,
hi and bye, itch and subjugation. Like chickens
that can distinguish fifty shades of yellow
in their feed, this one surely can distinguish
fifty shades of eyeliner and lip balm, just as I,
not to be outdone by one so young and graphic,
can distinguish fifty purpling shades of souring grape.

THREE CLOCKMAKERS FIX MY CLOCK

> *Time. Time. What is time? The Swiss manufacture it. The French hoard it. The Italians squander it. The Americans say it is money. The Hindus say it does not exist. Me? I say time is a crook.*
> —Truman Capote

The Swiss manufacture it.

Past months of escalating words
He swore I'd have it on the third.
Imagine my surprise whereon
He'd flown the second to Lausanne.
When he returned and found me waiting,
Livid, righteous, fibrillating,
I put my hands around my clock
And cursed him and his alpenstock.
You steal my work! He irate said.
You stole my time. So droppeth dead.

The Americans say that it is money.

What is time to a clockmaker?
Nothing sequential to Franklin,
For whom time stopped—
His legs were lopped.
(Was I virus? Was I war?
Was it *I* who'd closed the door?)
Ticking seconds, mounting days,
Cherry casing, moral haze.
The square concave, exclusively reproducible by
Carter's Clock Glass of Nashville, Tennessee,
And the ormolu bezel
Meant squat to Franklin.

Junk it. It's worthless.
You can't slap a cripple
So I told him what it meant in spatial terms:
My mother's smile at 8:00 a.m.,
The buzzing jolt to a first grade day,
The itchy slacks and the boomalacka blazer,
The smell of coffee rising up the stairs.
Junk it.
On the midden where your leg bones lie?

The Hindus say it does not exist.

He fixed the clock
Velvet-voiced Aditya,
Stripping it, oiling it,
Bending the hands deftly
To the arc of the square concave,
Reassembling elements
For form, line, style, and the
Wish to add a footnote to the
Previously written page.
His heart was not in it.
His heart nor his soul
I can accept nothing.
I owe you. You fixed it.
Sir, enjoy your clock.
I owe you for the time.
He smiled, waving his hand.
His time was his own.

SCOURING

> *I'm at the point where I wouldn't mind scoring with a maid.*
> — Bill
> *I'm at the point where I wouldn't mind scouring with a maid.*
> — Harry

They've crossed that bridge a score of times,
Headed into Roslyn, off to bed,
Drunk as lords, Bill by Harry led,
Far from reason, fast approaching rhyme.

They've toasted old reunions at The Tombs.
Harry married, Bill was close to dead.
Then they flip-flopped. Who came out ahead
In the fey recessional of rooms?

Forty years of settled-in routine,
Forty years of work when all is said
And done producing in them that toward which they've sped.
Scoring? Scouring? Both prospects seem lean.

There's no one else with whom they'd rather clink:
Why chase the maid around the room instead
Of mouthing off at memories of the bed?
Reminiscence doesn't mean you think.

Two more brews—the limit. They don't tarry.
Can't wait to take a leak and clear the head.
Last call. O'er the bridge they've fled,
Where each of them the other has to carry.

RESURRECTION

On top at last, at last l'amour!
Passionately clothes strewn on the floor.
Rest, my dear, no need to hurry on,
I'm going to the clinic, to Doctor Won.

The note you leave—*Thanks for hanging out*—
Removes from me the last, the teeniest shred of doubt.
You loved me truly, deeply, as I did you,
Sweet talk, no cash, dim sum, one game of pool.

And if I flag because of the events
It's not your fault—let's blame concupiscence.
How apt that you, a pro at coming close,
Should wittingly or not administer the dose.

I'll love you more than love is difficult
Six months from now, depending on results.

ALCATRAZ

One man called it the worst night of
the year, when he and the rest of the men
in isolation in the cold west wing caught
drifting through the bars, through a sieve
of stars—trumpets, trombones, kettles,
a flute's trill, the lilt of women giggling,
and he wondered what it would be like to
walk down any old street in California.

Come dawn and New Year's, while glancing
down from the refectory, he glimpsed a girl,
the first he'd seen in years, and he talked
of her, her hands, her shawl, the twining of
the violet rays of asters on her skirt, what he
took to be a modest hesitation in her step.
He wondered if she could be his sister, but
she was like no one he had ever seen or hoped
to see again. The cook then told him to shut up,
and when the girl looked up, her face, blameless,
chilled him. He stepped back, stepped forth, but she
had already slid beneath him into the prison yard.

FROZEN POSE

There you stand, in frozen pose,
1985, before the sea.
Everything things ever meant to me
Rooted in the wriggling of your toes.

Slightly knock-kneed, with hands on hips,
Scamp, the grin of pleasure broken out,
Break into your prance; resume your rout
Of me, spit of laughter on your lips.

Get me back there. I will shoot the clocks.
Knowing what I know, I'd quick go back
To my cherub. There I nothing lacked.
O my baby, you were like a rock.

Life since then has steadily grown cold.
You, however, never will be old.

WHITE CHRISTMAS

The card you sent
telling of your melanoma,
white sky, white trees on a
white field, white flakes
blanketing everything,
is the only card,
as I survey the lineup
on the mantelpiece,
blurred and buried in the
whited out woodwork,
that appears to be fading.

Inside, crabbed script—
*sorry to inflict this on you,
looming yearlong chemo,
time to get together.*

Yearlong I'll accept,
for in the implication that
you, who woke once
to bottles under the bed,
flashing on a crash
while raising Jen
cigarette by cigarette
till your heart seized—
you, who know death
better than anyone,
have got a chance to cheat her,
the trees bloom.

I accept.
Let's get together.
Cheat her.
You deserve the
blessings of the season.

AND OUR BRAINS HAVE SAILED AWAY

And our brains have sailed away,
What used to make us tick.
Is it luck or a roundelay
In an endless Stooges flick?

What used to make us tick
Was the mark of a cultured mind.
Not the endless Stooges flick
Where your forebrain's your behind.

In the dark of a cluttered mind,
Curly and Larry and Moe,
Where your forebrain's your behind
In the culture's afterglow.

Curly, Larry, Moe,
Nature's pentimenti.
In the culture's afterglow
The current cognoscenti.

Nature's pentimenti.
Who says we're out of luck,
The current cognoscenti?
Nyuk nyuk nyuk nyuk nyuk.

Who says we're out of luck?
Is it luck or a roundelay?
Nyuk, nyuk, nyuk, nyuk, nyuk—
And our brains have sailed away.

EVEN MORE LIMERICKS

It helps when your thoughts start to roam
To think about writing a poem.
The mind's interstices
Can feature Ulysses
Or someone much closer to home.

When your choice is the gentlemen's club
Or the standard American pub
If you don't have the leavage
To stuff in the cleavage
You'd best stick to burgers for grub.

My pastor will think it is odd of me
But I get a kick out of sodomy.
It's simply a fact
That the odder the act
The more it elicits the nod of me.

Free verse is a waste of our time.
To me what makes metrics sublime
Is the certain sensation
In versification
Of prosody rhymed on a dime.

MAGRITTE'S PALINDROME

Il a Dada, mon ami, no? T. S. Eliot is a tomato. My my! *Mot à mot!* As I toilest on I'm a nomad, a Dali.

SOPHISTICATED COURTSHIP PALINDROME

Evolution: dog, otter, a man on amaretto—God? No. I *tu* love.

PHILANDERER'S PALINDROME

Wow! Sir, I—O did I!—did Lily, Lil, Ada, Ava, Eve, Anna, Hannah, Nan, Anita, Nina, Tina, Nan, Hannah, Anna, Eve, Ava, Ada, Lily, Lil, Didi, Dido, Iris. Wow!

DE TROOT

Said the jackass to the bear,
I knows you lyin' there.
While I's around you'll please propound
De troot.

Said the Bear to Jack,
Trust is what you lack.
For umpteen years I tellin' you
De troot.

Jack reply to Bear,
Don't think it unfair,
But how do gibberish add up to
De troot?

Then the Bear come back
And up and say to Jack,
I combine de beaut
Wit de troot.

IT'S DONE, THE PLACE IS STRIPPED

It's done, the place is stripped.
Bedding, pillows, pictures,
Book and word, ancient, crumbling fixtures,
All but memory, waiting to be flipped.

The old linoleum gouged and cut,
Stainless door pulls misaligned and cracked,
The stopped clock, stripped, hacked
From the crotch where granite countertops abut.

The bed you died in vanished in thin air,
The couch they couldn't get out through the door.
Lying there, I'd hoped for something more.
Requiescat's less than hearty fare.

The scarparielli's walls, uncracked, uncleft,
Brooding on their weep holes, all that's left.

BARGEMAN

He used to watch the lighters and the bargemen in
our small town near Oneonta, feeling as we all did
that there was sense at the bottom of it. Of course
we were wrong. It was just the ebb and flow of
some things on the river, gray-bottomed, squared-off
dredgers, darting motorcraft, a punt, an occasional
scull propelled by a college kid from Binghamton,
nothing majestic, nothing more.

He, though, looked like he was on to something,
as if some day a woman, or even a man, would
materialize from the flow and stand there critically
peering at him, him not knowing why or what she
represented, no one from his childhood, no one
from his dreams, no one from his elder years,
but there just the same.

Every day he watched for ten or twenty minutes,
then left as if he had kept an appointment which now
had to be postponed. Finally he died. He was old enough
and went in his sleep.

Few things change along the river. Few things interrupt
the flow. I suppose she could show up now, but there is
less chance someone would know what to make of her.
I could, though I maintain hope that someday someone
will take his place.

TOO FEW

Too few
Kisses from you
Turn my ruddy blood blue.
I want to see your new tattoo—
Big time! Close up! *Hourly!* It's part of who
May someday trip as I pursue.
May all your dreams come true.
And mine for you
Come due.

THE BEAUTIFUL ERROR

tHIS MEANS jAKE,
sWIFT, HARRIED,
wHO READ
sTRUNK AND wHITE,
pOURED IT DOWN THE PAGE
wITHOUT LOOKING UP.
tAP, TAP, TAP. hE
tHOUGHT IT LETTER-PERFECT,
tHEN TAPPED A KEY
aND e-MAILED ME.
i SEE HOPE
iN ONE MAN'S
bLIND INSISTENCE ON
cAPITALIZATION.
hE HAS CONCURRED
iN AN ERROR. wHAT
a BEAUTIFUL ERROR
hE HAS MADE.

BATH

Every night I bathe in words,
soaping my armpits with adverbs,
squeezing a loofah full of pronouns over my head,
spritzing myself with vowels.
I love rubbing consonants over my chest,
lathering up my privates in fricatives and diphthongs,
rinsing off words like *very* and *hopefully*.
Sometimes I dive into a vat of adjectives,
break for the surface euphuistically,
wriggling through adjuncts and ablatives,
toweling off reluctantly,
already looking forward to the next bath.

UNTIL YOU SEDUCE A LESBIAN YOU'LL NEVER BE UPDIKE

He fancied the truck.
There's something about it,
he said, filling his lungs
as if we were headed out to sea.
It's a truck, I said.
It's real, he replied.
What's real is the world of words, I said.
A truck is a toy made by kids who
want to drive one.
You wouldn't say that if you were me,
he said.
But you'd say it if you were me, I
replied.
We hopped into the cab and headed down
the street.
I could tell he thought it was real,
the noise, the power, the height
and visibility.
He was wrong, though. It really was
a toy made by kids wanting to drive one.
You're wrong, he said, rolling down the window.
Words are vapor. This is real.
Bob, I said, just try harder.
Until you seduce a lesbian you'll never be Updike.

THE RETURN OF MADAME LA HOYA

> *Boss, she don't have the money. Then tell Madame La Hoya she isn't going to hoya anymore.*
>
> — Preston Sturges

I can see her there where the breeze parts the lace,
gazing insanely at the cards—*Tarrot*'s the spelling
on the sign—past the jowls of the fat girl searching
for the Larry embedded in the Larry she wound up with.
I don't know my fate, but Sandra does at Sandra's
Palm & Card Parlor.

I want with a straight face to pay her.
I want with a straight face to ask her,
What is the capitol of North Dakota?
Like the time my dad advised me to buy
life insurance and I was twenty and I thought,
what a stupid idea, coughing up eighteen
bucks a month of very important beer money
so that my baronial holdings can be forked
over to creditors should my Chevy shoot over
a cliff.

So when the insurance guy asked me if I smoked,
I told him I never stop smoking, and when he
asked how much I drank I said *two quarts a day.*
When I started hypoventilating from my morning
dose of opium and sank to the floor in grand mal,
the insurance guy departed and dad said to me,
I wish you years of uninterrupted health.

I can't explain the urge to talk to Sandra. Perhaps
I miss my dad and his advice. The hell with love,
here's what I want to know. When will I murder Paul?
Can a medium order steak rare? Why is your clientele
fat? Am I headed to heaven or hell? What ever happened
to the insurance guy? When will I fuck a Brazilian?—
tell me if *that's* in the cards. Oh, forget it, Sandra. I
don't need to know. If I live to be a hundred, what
will I do for suspense?

About the Author

Fired from Hallmark for writing meaningful greeting-card verse, he once ran twenty straight balls at pool; finished 183rd (out of about 10,000) at the 1985 U.S. Open Crossword Puzzle Tournament; won a yodeling contest in a German restaurant; was bitten by a guard dog in a tattoo parlor; survived a car crash with Sidney Lumet; Paul Newman once claimed to have known him for a long time; hasn't been arrested in 17 months.

About NYQ Books™

NYQ Books™ was established in 2009 as an imprint of The New York Quarterly Foundation, Inc. Its mission is to augment the *New York Quarterly* poetry magazine by providing an additional venue for poets already published in the magazine. A lifelong dream of NYQ's founding editor, William Packard, NYQ Books™ has been made possible by both growing foundation support and new technology that was not available during William Packard's lifetime. We are proud to present these books to you and hope that you will continue to support The New York Quarterly Foundation, Inc. and our poets and that you will enjoy these other titles from NYQ Books™:

Joanna Crispi	*Soldier in the Grass*
Ted Jonathan	*Bones and Jokes*
Amanda J. Bradley	*Hints and Allegations*
Ira Joe Fisher	*Songs from an Ealier Century*
Kevin Pilkington	*In the Eyes of a Dog*

Please visit our website for these and other titles:

www.nyqbooks.org